As I Walk

A collection of original poems and short stories

by

Diane Neilson

As I Walk

Copyright © 2025 Diane Neilson

All rights reserved.

ISBN: 9798292210900

DEDICATION

To my children and grandchildren.

May you always follow your dreams and find the right path.

As I Walk

May Day	49
A Dandy Adventure	51
Mayflower Whiteout	54
It's Beginning to Look a lot like Springtime	56
Spring is Here	58
Camino	59
Found	60
Serendipity	61
The Gift of a Breeze	62
Slow Walking	63
Betwixt	64
If	66
September Rain	68
Autumn is Here	69
When Life gets Messy	70
Colours of Autumn	76
The Nothing Day	77
November's Nuance	78
A Prayer	79
The Old Oak	81
Nature's Rainbow	82
The School Run	83
Tick Tock	84
The Shroud	90
When Life gives me Lemons	92
Hamstrung in December	93
Snow Days	95
A Child's Voice	97

As I Walk

CONTENTS

As I Walk *part 1*	3
The Goyt is Closed	4
January Rains	6
Starters for Tea	7
A Different Way	9
Snow	10
Big Coats	11
Purpose	12
Dawn Walk	17
I think it's Going to Rain Today	18
Mad March	20
Walking with Friends	21
Blue Sky Hope	22
Nature's Prayer	23
The Song Thief	24
Awake with the Birds	25
Nature's Bounty	30
Be Gentle with Yourself	32
The Storm Rages	33
4 Reasons to Cycle	34
Who are You?	35
The Rental	37
Breathe	39
Saturday Night Fever	41
Hide and Seek	48

As I Walk

Winter	99
Martyr	100
The Dance of the Sugar Plum Fairy	102
The Boggart	113
Wisp 'o' the Wold	117
As I Walk *part 2*	120
About the Author	123

As I Walk

As I Walk *part 1*

As I walk my mind is freed
From dull responsibility
From angst and negativity
        Forgotten as I walk

The stomach clenching knot released
As heartbeat syncs with tread of feet
Yet mind continues, unpoliced
           and lightens as I walk

The corners of my mind spring-cleaned
I reclaim long forgotten dreams
To contemplate those fairy queens
           and kingdoms, as I walk

My eyes, unblinkered, see the world
The foxglove blooms, the fern unfurls
The swallow swoops on breeze that swirls
           caressing, as I walk

My ears are tuned to streams that babble
Darting fish, a falling apple
As thoughts converge, ideas merge,
           possess me as I walk

Across the stile and down the hill
I hurry home, my book to fill
To capture words with loaded quill
           collected as I walk

The Goyt is closed

The Goyt is closed, no path ahead!
You cannot pass, the notice said
The storm has wreaked it havoc true
The way is closed for me and you

"But is it?" My enquiring mind
has questions of the defiant kind
Where there's a will there's usually a way
I'll make up my own mind, if I do say

Not a soul did I see on the path
Which in parts resembled a rural bath
But the squirrels still searched and the birds still darted
Unperturbed and ever light hearted

With trees uprooted and branches broken
the storm and its winds had clearly spoken
But now there is peace and the air is quite still
The landscape redrawn at the artist's will

A swollen torrent fills the ravine
Where once meandered a trickling stream
Hurried along with astonishing force
As if impatient to fulfil its course.

At last I reach the broken bridge
A sorry sight but a temporary hitch
A stream to cross, a bank to clamber
then back on track, the woods to wander

As I Walk

I probably shouldn't have followed that trail
The notice was clear and the bridge 'had' failed
But I'm glad I tasted the forbidden pleasure
For it made more delicious the woodlands treasures

January Rains

January, wet and windy

Gone the December indecisiveness
Replaced by the certainty of a daily squall
Long rambles replaced by short hurried walks
Shoehorned in between the showers

Rivulets of rain coat the window
Drops converging to run their course
Gutters overflowing, storm drains lifted,
As water seeks lower ground flooding all in its path

The garden lies untended, wild
But becomes an oasis for birds, calling as they search for food
Unperturbed by the weather's rage
Joyful in their reborn freedom

The moorland is unpassable
A boggy wasteland seeping and oozing
Ravines have become rivers and the reservoir is, at last, full
As water courses down the hillside

Rain, the saviour of our planet
Water-table raised; lakes filled to the brim
The sheep continue to graze and the birds will always sing
To celebrate the January rain

Starters for Tea

When my children came home from their grandma's, to me
They talked about having picnics for tea
A rug on the carpet in front of the fire
Whilst all still wearing school uniform attire

A tiny triangular sandwich with ham

A cracker with cheese and a half-scone with jam

A handful of crisps and some apple in pieces

Grapes cut in half and white chocolate 'meeces'

Tellytubby toast and cherry tomatoes

Crispy french-fries made from baby potatoes

Cold chopped up sausage or cubed chicken tikka

Then on the settee to watch Tracy Beaker

But now they're all grown up, and when they all visit
they'll ask, "what's for tea, is it hot pot or brisket?"
If there isn't much in, or they can't all agree
Then I'll often suggest, "Let's have starters for tea!"

Jalapeno poppers with sweet chilli sauce

And crispy calamari, with mayo of course

As I Walk

Olives and hummus and warm pitta bread

And tomatoes with feta, all sundried and red

Salt 'n' pepper crisps, a bagful to share

A leftover slice of rump steak, cooked rare

Chorizo with mushrooms and lemon to squeeze

You can't do much better than 'starters for tea'.

A Different Way

I didn't have much time today, so I took my feet a different way.
A local park I don't usually frequent, with new things to see, it was time well spent.

The rainclouds of earlier spent or moved on, a breeze in the air and a hint of the sun.
A swan with her cygnet, all white fluff and down.
And three ducks: one mallard, one white and one brown.

The weather was breezy and really quite cool, the park full of children on half term from school.
Grannies and grandads, sisters and brothers, dog-walkers a plenty all greeting each other.
Despite the cool morning the ice-cream van was busy,
Serving cornets and sprinkles and sherbert - all fizzy.

With blackbirds and robins competing in song, I just didn't want to be hurried along.
So I dillied and dallied enjoying the scene, a pleasant encounter I hadn't foreseen.
And my day carried on with jobs still to do, but refreshed by a simple walk somewhere quite new.

So next time you're busy or time's a bit short, go for a walk of a different sort.
You never know what you'll see the day that you let your feet take you a different way.

Snow

The transformative magic of a snowy day

Erasing all signs of yesterday's January

A blanket of white reimagines the day

As a beautiful playground, a wonderland sanctuary

Monochrome tones have whitewashed the land

A ghostly blizzard shrouds the hill in white

Peace has descended, silence its command

The light remains low and dusk will come early tonight

Light the fire and turn the lamps down low

With luck, tonight, it will snow, snow, snow

Big Coats

"Put on your big coats and go out to play!"

Said my mam on a freezing February day.

"But mam, it's cold, and those clouds look like rain.

Can't we just light the fire, stay inside, play a game?"

"You're under my feet and I can't get 'owt done;

I've the washing to do and the tea to get on.

You're not made of sugar, and won't blow away,

so put on your big coats and go out to play."

Purpose

Betty is searching for meaning at a time in her life when she is feeling slightly redundant. In this short story, she is directed by nature towards a new and purposeful chapter.

"There she goes again."

They didn't know then that she was a 'she', but something about her waddling walk reminded them of a busy woman about her business.

It was 4pm on a late afternoon in May, and Alf and Betty were sitting in the summer house, camping heater on and hot cups of tea in hand, trying to pretend that summer had arrived, whilst a chill breeze swept over Pendle Hill behind them.

They watched as the huge hedgehog clambered out from behind the vegetable bed, scurried across the path and disappeared behind next door's shed - an action replay of last night, and every other night, for the last couple of weeks.

It was lovely to see, but it did present them with a bit of a dilemma.

Hedgehogs were becoming somewhat of a rarity - even in rural Lancashire - so they were thrilled to be seeing one so frequently in the garden. However, as hedgehogs are more usually seen at dusk, they were a little worried seeing her out in broad daylight so often, and all of the online information Alf had found said that a hedgehog out in daylight is a hedgehog in trouble, and that help should be sought by taking it to a rescue centre.

"Go and get that cardboard box out of the spare room and I'll run it up to Tiggywinkles," he said.

Betty hesitated. "I don't want to. I like her being here. Let's just keep our eye on her for a few more days," she suggested hopefully.

Unused to being challenged, Alf stood up dramatically, hands in the air. "On your "ead be it then. Don't come crying to me if it all ends in tears."

Betty now felt unsure. What if Alf was right and something terrible happened? Maybe they should just do as he said.

But for some reason, instinct held her back. The hedgehog was large, moving well, seemed purposeful, and was obviously keeping a routine, so she decided to hold her ground; to watch and wait.

The hedgehog's routine continued, monitored closely by Betty, and about a week later, with the weather much improved, she was sitting lower down in the garden on the patio, G&T in hand and enjoying a book and the sunshine.

Alf was inside, as he had been since the disagreement the previous week, choosing to read his newspaper and do his crossword alone.

A sudden rustling directed Betty's attention to the foliage below, and before her very eyes, the hedgehog climbed up over the low wall and began to follow what was clearly her usual route, around the perimeter of the garden and up through the vegetable patch, before crossing the path and disappearing, as usual, behind next door's shed.

Beside herself with excitement, Betty rushed inside to tell Alf, thrilled to have found out a little more of the hedgehog's routine and eager to share the news.

Reluctantly, on hearing the news, Alf allowed himself to be persuaded to venture out for a look, but all was quiet.

"For goodness' sake Betty, stop dragging me out for nothing. Haven't you got anything better to do than sit waiting for wildlife to appear?"

Dismayed, she realised she didn't - have anything better to do, that is.

She hadn't realised how dull her days had become since their youngest had left home; how unimportant the cooking and cleaning suddenly felt.

It didn't seem to have had the same impact on Alf, he still had his mates at work and the darts team twice a week - nothing had really changed for him, and she felt like the paper and crossword took priority once he got home.

A little later, Betty was sitting in the garden, mulling all this over whilst nursing a coffee. When had she started to feel like this?

Deflated, but not put off, she had maintained her watch, the excitement and anticipation brightening up her days for the rest of the week and giving her something to look forward to each day.

Absentmindedly, she watched as the yellow flowers of the shrub nodded somewhat more vigorously than usual. Suddenly alert, she cocked her head and listened. She hadn't seen the hedgehog for a few days now and somewhat deflated, had begun to prepare herself for the reality of another wave of empty nest syndrome.

What she was not prepared for, was the sight of a tiny snout emerging from the Dahlias. Quietly, she edged closer to the wall, peering over it into the dark tangle of the undergrowth below, and as she watched, not one, not two, not even three, but four tiny hoglets shuffled out from the gloomy shade into the sunlight to root around in the detritus, obviously looking for food.

Elation immediately turned to panic. Where was the mother? What if they couldn't look after themselves? What if they tumbled to their death? The ledge where they had emerged from was atop the precipice of a five foot stone wall.

Heart in her mouth, Betty ran inside to share the news - and the sudden responsibility of a whole new family - with Alf.

He wasn't there. Of course he wasn't, it was Friday - darts night, and he wouldn't be back until 9pm which could well be too late.

In a panic, Betty made a snap decision. She would drive up to Tiggywinkles herself and ask their advice.

As she snatched up her handbag and the car keys, she tried to ignore the nagging voice in her head telling her that she hadn't driven for over five years; not since she reversed into next door's wall and ruined Mabel's favourite rose bush. Alf had said that she should leave the driving to him after that, and she hadn't argued.

But this was an emergency! Holding her breath, she started the engine and reversed out of the drive - so far so good.

As she headed out of town, she began to relax. "I can do this!" she thought, a tiny seed of self-belief lodging itself in her mind.

A few minutes later, up by the reservoir, she pulled into the driveway and onto the carpark of the animal sanctuary. As she entered the building and approached the enquiry desk, her attention was drawn to a notice board and a poster, displaying a photograph of a family of hedgehogs. Underneath was a notice,

"Volunteers Needed"

Could you give a few hours a week to help this little family and others like them?"

Slowly, Betty smiled. She had found what she was looking for - Purpose.

Dawn Walk

A walk alone, a wakeful meditation
Unhurried thoughts wander freely
A morning yet untarnished, the day to come, full of promise

Dawn has delivered a perfect sky
Emerald grass glistening with dew
The voice of the breeze and the song of the babbling brook

The early light is different somehow
Bright yet gentle, colouring the hills
Untainted by the harsh rays of the midday sun

Empty footpaths free the mind
A new view to reawaken imagination
Inspiration, rarely sought but often gained

Breathing in the cool air
Allowing its pureness to cleanse my soul
Nourishment from Mother Nature

Your own pace, your own direction
Questions asked, options considered
Perspective gained. At peace. Ready for the day

I Think It's Going to Rain Today

I think it's going to rain today.
Should I pull on my boots or put them away?
I could put on my slippers, sit by the grate,
warming my fingers and toes 'til it's late.

I think it's going to rain today,
Shall I discard my raincoat? Stay out of the grey?
I could finish my book, enjoy biscuits and tea,
make a hotpot for dinner - apple crumble maybe.

I could catch up on chores, give my mum a quick call,
bake cookies, write a haiku, knit a scarf, paint the hall.
I could have a long bath, watch a film, yes I may!
I can do all these things if I stay in today.

But if I go out, if I pull on my boots,
I may see a Woodpecker, Kestrel or Coot.
The Robins and Finches would brighten my day,
so maybe I won't put my fell boots away.

Because when I get out there'll be no-one around,
no footsteps to hear just that rain-dropping sound.
The trees will be silent, the water so still,
just me and my thoughts and the cows on Calf Hill.

And when I return, I can still do those things,
The chores and the calls and the hobbies, food and drinks.
And after a shower, and soup in a mug,
with my boots and coat drying I'll be feeling quite smug.

As I Walk

I think it's going to rain today,
I'll pull on my boots and walk anyway.

Mad March

Wind howling and loosening tiles, the rain has wiped out everyone's smiles.

A dark grey sky and scuttling clouds

Is it November, or March?

Pale blue sky and a watery sun, warm enough to think spring has begun.

Daffodils nodding their heads contentedly.

Is it June, or March?

Frosty rooftops and skating rink streets, clouds of icy breath and freezing feet.

The clear sky and blossom show their deceit!

Is it still winter, or Spring?

Walking With Friends

Walking with friends
The usual trails, mist hanging in the air
Views hidden, cloud descending to surround us
Goes unnoticed

We talk as we walk
Through grass and mud, over field and stile
Months of memories and news to share
The light fades

Mud becomes tarmac
The pub is in sight and warmth awaits us
Good food, a roaring fire, glasses raised
Why do we leave it so long?

Blue Sky Hope

When the lane up the hill is more puddle than path, and you're up to your ankles in mud;
when the stream overflows and is running so fast that it almost resembles a flood.
Look out for the signs that the dark days are passing and think what the future could bring.
For a milky, blue sky and a chill wind, send reminders of winter, but the promise of spring.

When faces are surly, turned stony with cold, and warm greetings are mumbled at best;
the skeletal trees stand defiant and proud, for their memories are strong, not repressed.
As the cormorants dive and the skylarks perform, you just want to join in with their fling.
For a blue sky and a chill wind, raise our spirits somehow and prepare us for spring.

In the field there's a bleating from near and afar, as the new lambs embrace their new world;
and ahead in the meadow, a slight hint of green as the leaves of the hawthorn unfurl.
The robins and blackbirds begin to collect moss and grasses and twigs, as they sing.
The chill wind is forgotten and blue sky wins out, with its message of Hope, and of spring.

Nature's Prayer

A peachy sky as the sun is rising
Snowdrops thrive and crocus' bloom
The promise of a perfect day
Emerging from the winter's gloom

A hint of blue in a porcelain sky
Warmth in battle with the chill of the breeze
Weak spring sunshine breaking through
Inviting birdsong and the first of the bees

The river swollen, gushing downstream
Blackthorn blooms as winter closes
Robins and blackbirds spring into action
Winter fades as Spring proposes

Wobbly lambs at their mother's udder
The sound of bleating fills the air
Spring is on its way again
Answering nature's silent prayer

The Song Thief

Where are the birds on a blustery day?
The wind has stolen their voices away
The lambs are still bleating, the cattle still low
But where is the birdsong? Where did it go?

Was it carried up high in the Sycamore tree?
Or lost to the brook as it babbled downstream?
Did it follow the moon to sit with the stars?
Where is the birdsong? Has it gone far?

There was no goodbye, they were here yesterday
The Blackbirds and Robins, the Thrush and the Jay
Chirping and trilling, their songs full of joy
An abundance of beautiful, glorious noise

When dawn breaks tomorrow, I hope it is still
That the wind holds its fury, though I bear it no ill
That the breeze will be gentle and not steal away
The voice of the songbirds which brighten each day

Awake with the Birds

News of sadness and suffering around the world can sometimes make us feel helpless and frustrated, but a walk in nature can help us to regain perspective and balance in our life.

She awoke early.

She had dozed into an easy slumber around midnight, lulled by the soothing call of the Tawny Owl in the field behind the house, but from about 4am she had slept restlessly, her right hip aching and her mind racing. It was the news that haunted her, the children in particular; their little tear-streaked faces, the dirty drinking water, the flies – especially the flies! And then, in the next report, bombs being dropped on those same families; grief-stricken mothers, whole families homeless – or lost; boys fighting boys, and for what? All in the name of power or religion.

Religion! She was pretty sure that Jesus wouldn't have approved of all this fighting.

It was no use, there was no sleep in her so she might as well get up and do something useful. The cat was pleased – an early breakfast and cuddle – but she still couldn't settle. She needed to walk.

She crept back upstairs, stealthily avoiding the creaky fourth stair and the squeaky floorboard on the landing. She scooped up yesterday's clothes and hurriedly dressed before re-navigating the descent in reverse and pulling on her boots and coat.

When she opened the back door, it was still dark, the moon dipping over the hill at the back of the house and the sky clear, a light breeze whipping at her hair. She crossed the bridge over the brook and began to trudge up the lane, just one foot in front of another trying to shake the feeling of frustration that all was not right with the world.

A rustle ahead dragged her out of her depressing contemplation. A shadow, right in front of her. No sooner had she identified it than it leapt the wall – a deer, no more than a fawn, and it had clearly not expected to see her at this early hour. Just a baby and no mother in sight. Why couldn't people live like wildlife, side by side in harmony? She knew it was not that simple and that there was plenty 'war' in nature, but it wasn't the same. It wasn't driven by power-mad, money-hungry individuals; rich people trying to get richer at everyone else's expense and narcissists who all wanted to be 'King of the world', it was simply survival.

The sun was starting to rise now, a glorious tangerine and rose sky developing like a photograph in front of her. As though synchronised, a morse code of birdsong broke the silence signalling the start of the new day, and despite her feelings about the world, she felt the malaise slip from her shoulders as though a weight had been lifted.

She turned off the lane at the foot of the moor and continued uphill, the cows in the lower field eyeing her curiously before returning to their grazing. Crossing the stile, she passed through reed-beds, the path unseasonally dry for April, and continued up to the woods above the reservoir, where the trail became twisty and narrow. She crossed a stile to follow a path she hadn't walked before, beside a fast-running stream that tumbled down the hillside over rocks like a mini-waterfall. After a few minutes she was in the midst of the woods with only the birds for company. She sat on a boulder, suddenly needing to just be at one with nature, and closed her eyes.

The birds were now in full song; the blackbirds shouting their orders, chaffinches trilling a morning tune and the glorious melody of the song thrush reaching her ears in intricate bursts, from the uppermost branch of the oak tree.

She continued on her path, the warning call of the Robin offending her somewhat – she was no threat to them!

Reaching the edge of the moor and crossing the stile, she began the gentle sloping descent. Marsh pipits darted in and out of the heather, whilst curlews glided lazily above her – how wonderful it must be to just soar high above the world, drifting on the breeze, being carried along by the thermals – no wonder they sang.

At the stream she stopped to watch the dipper, the white flash of his breast disappearing and then reappearing, emerging triumphant as he bobbed and searched for food amongst the rocks, water tumbling over him before he swept, glistening, into the trees above.

Through the gate, she was greeted by the horses, nosing in her pockets for apples or carrots. She apologised (the farmer had forbidden feeding) and gave them both a nose rub instead – obviously a poor replacement, as they wandered away to seek out fresh grass.

Suddenly something caught her eye; a flash of brown swooping down in the next field. She crept silently to the wall where she would be hidden from sight, eager to make the most of this rare, if yet unconfirmed, sighting. After a few moments of uncomfortable crouching, she made to move – she must have been mistaken. Then, from the lowland grasses, emerged a hen-harrier – a female, a ring-tale – claws empty, rising almost vertically into the sky. She watched frozen as it hovered, silent and still, before dropping again to earth, this time rising with a small mammal, maybe a vole or a shrew, and flying away into the woods. She wondered at its skill, its authority, its speed – a marvel of nature.

Strolling back down the footpath home, she mulled over what she had seen. Why was a hen-harrier a marvel of nature, despite being a ruthless killing machine, whilst human killing was a blatant atrocity? It was a contradiction that upset her, made her feel a hypocrite, and she wrestled with the discomfort all the way home, where she made a coffee and went to sit in the summer house.

From her vantage point in the garden there was plenty of entertainment; wrens and sparrows were darting in and out of the ivy, nest-building she supposed – it was that time of year; two nuthatches were shouting noisily to each other from the plum tree, and a parliament of rooks had gathered in the farthest sycamore. What were they debating, she wondered, they were certainly doing it noisily. Maybe they were discussing the hen-harrier's murderous behaviour.

She laughed to herself before rising to go back inside. The world was far from perfect, but as long as she had her garden, and the birds, she would just have to accept that the state of the world was beyond her control.

Maybe she would go and put a cheque in the 'Red

Cross' envelope that came last week – do her bit. Who knows, there may be a 'real' parliament in the world who could sort out the mess made by the billionaires and madmen, and if not, perhaps a real-life murderous equivalent of her hen-harrier was waiting in the wings to swoop down and take out the 'king-of-the-world'. An evil thought maybe, but she went in through the back door with a lighter heart and her fingers crossed.

Nature's Bounty

For how many years has this view been admired?
How many words and ideas inspired?
Which generation first noticed its splendour,
and how many since have observed its agenda?

Spring comes in secret as nature awakes,
and miniscule changes observe each daybreak
Then slowly but surely the blossom unfolds,
encouraging each flower to stand and be bold

As summer approaches, one senses a shift
The pace of life quickens as the temperature lifts
'Til before our own eyes is a riot of colour
and we bask in the joy of the long days of summer

A new autumn palette helps soften the blow,
turning forests ablaze in its own special show
No urgency now, just a hunkering down,
as the colours of summer turn first red, then brown

With a chill in the air, we feel winter's embrace,
and time seems to slow as the year ends its race
With the land and the sky bleached of colour and warmth,
a new world appears in its skeletal form

The earth sleeps and recovers through the ice and the snow,
conserving its energy, its bounty run low
Hiding its secret, and patient in slumber,
until the right time to reveal next year's wonder

Generations have passed but the cycle remains,
and with cameras we strive to record every change
But a picture can never portray what we see,
the magnificence of nature, abundant and free

Be Gentle with Yourself

Be busy at rest, allow your mind to still,
Remember times that caused your heart to sing;
Be gentle with yourself, be free.

Imagine the stories that the cloudy skies tell,
The pictures they form just to disperse again;
Be busy at rest, allow your mind to still.

Be at one with the birds, embrace their orchestral crescendo,
The rise and fall of the melody they create;
Be gentle with yourself, be free.

Let your mind float high on the breeze, like a feather,
Riding the thermals and obeying its direction without question;
Be busy at rest, allow your mind to still

Be watchful, 'but careless', for what you see is not yours,
Not your problem to solve, not today;
Be gentle with yourself, be free.

And as you sit, in peaceful contemplation,
Deny any thoughts and embrace meditation;
Be busy at rest, allow your mind to still,
Be gentle with yourself, be free.

The Storm Rages

It starts with a darkening, a lessening of blue as the grey gains the upper hand.
The sun retreats as her great rival approaches, not prepared to do battle today, not prepared for this fight.

Then the wind, a tornado descends, whirling the leaves from the ground.
The trees bend, their branches dragging trunks into unnatural poses, bowing to a greater force.

Rain starts softly, as if to trick you that you may escape the torrent to come.
Pitter-patter gains volume until water is being hurled from the raging black clouds of the storm.

Lightening cracks, thunder rolls, its voice at first distant, but creeping closer.
Until together they unite, overhead, a violent energy unleashed on the world.

As quickly as it starts, the storm is over, its energy spent, its rage subdued.
It creeps away, exhausted, leaving the gentle sound of summer rain to lull us to sleep.

4 Reasons to Cycle

Contemplation

    Reflection

        Nature

            Peace

Who are You?

Who are you? Have you ever thought?
And does it matter, your type, your sort?
How tiresome, demands that are placed on our race,
and constantly changing, young or old, place to place

Are you pleased or unhappy with what you are and have got?
Have you made some mistakes? Show me someone who's not!
Do you wish things were different - better somehow
Or does the constant change feel like a merry-go-round?

Are you too fat, too thin or are you just right;
too tall or too short, or just the right height;
straight hair or curly, blue eyes or brown:
fair skin or olive, face angled or round?

Too quiet, too loud, too humble, too proud;
are you busy or lazy, too quiet, too crazy?
Prefer animals to people or the other way round
Are your cogs always turning or is your head in the clouds?

A born fashionista or prefer comfy trainers?
Heels and a dress or are jeans a no-brainer?
Would you walk in the fields or stroll on a beach,
climb mountains, sail rivers, search things out of reach?

Would you shop in big cities, relax on a yacht,
search out trinkets and treasures, put money in slots?
Enjoy meeting people or prefer your close friends,

or enjoy your own company every weekend?

The life that you weave is the one you should love
It should shroud you in comfort and fit like a glove
It isn't, and shouldn't, determine your position,
should seek no apology nor invite inquisition
For you are just you, if you've ever thought
Ordinary yet special, a unique type or sort.

The Rental

White door. Plastic. No number.
New carpets over stone floors
Cracked paint on windowsill
90's radiators

New paint job on old wallpaper
Crumbling plaster lurks beneath
Uneven stairs, lethal gradient
Curtain rail broken

Outdated boiler newly stamped
Sink dulled with Brillo pad,
the shine worn off
And an old gas stove

Painted over tiles
And painted over mould
Original features – gone
Replaced with modern tat

Kitchen lino cut to fit
Blinds hotch-potch, made to do
Closed windows and musty air
And TWO fire extinguishers

Yard enclosed by old stone wall
Shabby, concrete square with broken panes
Dripping overflow pipe leaves a green trail down dirty render
Out-house still filled with crap – just a different kind

Dry, warm, ours
Evri-man delivers our home in boxes
Clean, polish, sweep, air
Our first house together
Home!

Breathe

I awake. I'm warm, comfortable, snug, the cat nestled in the crook of my left leg.
Dreams, already memories, are drifting in and out of my consciousness - hazy and incomplete.
But then the real memories return: the words, the shame, the guilt. Frustration most of all - I'm her mum! I should be able to fix this. Why can't I fix this?
Breathe.

I breakfast, not really tasting.
The murmurs inside my brain continue - won't be shaken - no logic can shift them. I need a walk.
I step out into the morning mist.
A sharp intake of breath cold on my lungs, a welcome release from thought.
The path up is hard, exactly what I need.
Breathe - in two, hold for two, out two.

At the top, a pause for breath.
It's going to rain. For a moment I am hypnotised by the sheet of rain moving along the valley, distant yet, but on its way.
I turn to follow the now familiar path.
Breath steadier, mind already calmer, I focus my mind on nature, on birdsong and the gurgle of water.
Breathe - in three, hold for three, out three.

As I Walk

A flock approaching, wary.
I stop, the sheep pass holding their nerve. I look back and their heads are held high - mine too.
Further on a calf nuzzles. The cow sleeps and the bull snorts his disapproval. Family dynamics for all to see. No shame, no guilt.

I pause at the bench and sit, looking out over the lake. A cormorant swoops and dives. The heron, like a statue at the edge - on guard.
The mist lifts revealing a fox on the edge of the woods, frozen in time. I close my eyes and count to ten. He's gone - was he ever there?
Breathe - in four, hold for four, out four.

Downhill now, dodging mud and puddles.
The last of the summer's blackberries sweet on my tongue.
The birdwatcher rounds the corner and we chat - a pipit and a skylark so far this morning; I tell him about the cormorant.
The rain arrives - I knew it would - washing away the words, the shame, the guilt.
We are just people. I am doing my best. She is doing her best.
Breathe.

Saturday Night Fever

When feels like life has turned against you and everything is going wrong, often it is the kindness of ordinary people and the humour in everyday events that can get you through.

It was Saturday night, 8.30pm and they were in A&E. Triple whammy - a situation nobody wants to find themselves in - ever! It was going to be a tough night.

To be honest it had already been a tough day, and for Tony a tough week. He had caught the blasted cold from his wife last weekend, and whilst she had endured a grotty couple of days before gradually improving, he had got steadily worse, and by Friday he had needed to call the doctors, something he avoided if at all possible.

He returned dejectedly from an emergency appointment with a packet of antibiotics for a chest infection, hopeful at least, that this time tomorrow he would be on the mend. By the next afternoon, showing no improvement - in fact feeling decidedly worse - they had called 111 and the advisor (after what felt like hundreds of questions) had made them an appointment with an on-call doctor, who had, in turn, promptly packed them off to hospital. So here they were, and it was a madhouse!

Tony sat down whilst Diane checked him in. He felt panicky, breathless and more than a little nauseous, and all this noise wasn't helping one bit. Fortunately, because he had been referred, he was triaged immediately and taken to a side room where he was wired up to a monitor. He sat back and closed his eyes, trying to will the awful feelings to go away.

Diane was frantic and trying not to show it. She had been short with the on-call doctor, questioning his opinions (the only useful thing he had said was to go to hospital), and then she had got them lost, ending up at the hospital's mental health facility instead of A&E. After frantically driving round for ten minutes, she had abandoned the car next to an ambulance to get Tony inside, almost screamed at the automated check-in machine's inane questions, and then had to abandon him whilst she went to find the car park and park the car. Just to add another layer of stress, when she returned, he had disappeared from where she'd left him; if a friendly nurse hadn't noticed her panic and taken her to the side room where he was being monitored, they would probably have had to cart *her* off, back to that mental facility they passed earlier.

When she walked in, Tony looked calm - lay on the bed and hooked up to the monitors. She composed herself before speaking.
"Are you feeling any better, love?"
"Not so bad," he murmured, without opening his eyes.

He was lying. She knew he must be feeling terrible. He was a brave man who hated hospitals and this was his worst nightmare - their worst nightmare. She sat on the bed beside him and held his hand. Helplessness is a terrible feeling and she was totally at a loss as to what she could do to make him feel better. She had hoped that the on-call doctor would just

As I Walk

give him a new prescription, not this! It was going to be a long night.

It was actually quite promising in the beginning. Initial observations complete, they were ushered through to 'Majors' to speak to a doctor. Majors was mayhem on another scale, with a long queue of trolleys and their miserable incumbents lining the corridor, a group of police officers restraining a furious looking man, and a huge number of people constantly bustling around.
Because Tony was being monitored, they were shown into a side room - a sparse, white box, but luxury compared to the corridor. Not long after, a nurse arrived, telling them that the doctor was looking at the test results and would be along shortly with a plan. It sounded like good news; they weren't going to be home for Strictly, but it didn't sound like it would be too long.

But there are obviously different rules about time in hospitals, because 'shortly' still hadn't arrived and it was now midnight. As Tony alternated between coughing and dozing, Diane was left to watch the monitor, feeling waves of dread followed by relief as the numbers went up and down. Tony clearly wasn't out of the woods yet and she was desperate for the doctor to walk through the door with a plan to make all this go away.

Ignoring the hateful, beeping machine, she focused on the corridor. Trolleys were wheeled past with all manner of occupants, some bleeding, some crying, others still and silent which seemed worse for some reason. An army of health workers in a whole array of different uniforms marched up and down the corridor, in and out of rooms, pushing trolleys, taking machines and medicine and all manner of 'equipment' wherever it was needed.

Worried families followed the trolleys or stood by the beds in the corridor, trying to give comfort and support; one woman was also looking after the man on the next trolley, fixing his blanket for him and passing him paper tissues.

A worrying number of police officers were visible, escorting people back and forth along the corridor, it made Diane wonder about what sort of Saturday night 'fun' people got up to nowadays.

At around 2am, and after another check by the nurse (still no doctor), Diane turned the light off and pushed the door to. Tony was dozing, his mouth wide open and making little gasping noises. The machine was bleeping incessantly and an alarm was going off somewhere.

She leaned her head back against the wall and closed her eyes, trying to zone out the noise. Horrible dark thoughts kept popping into her head, nasty little gremlins dropping nightmare scenarios that she couldn't push away; she felt as though she was going out of her mind. Rising sharply, she left the room and crossed the corridor to the bathroom. There was a large smear of blood on the wall. She felt sick.
She washed her face with cold water only to discover that there were no paper towels in the dispenser, and made her way, dripping miserably, back to the room.

Tony was awake. "I need a wee," he said sheepishly. "Oh, " exclaimed Diane, "well I'm not sure how we're going to get you to the bathroom with all your - adornments. We'd better call the nurse."

Once the situation had been explained, the nurse brought a cardboard bottle, placing it on the bed before leaving with a breezy, "Press the button when you're done." Tony and Diane looked uncertainly at each other. Tony was lay on the bed fully clothed in jeans and a jumper, with a drip in one arm and a blood pressure cuff on the other, an oxygen tube was draped over his shoulder and up into his nose and several wires were attached to his person.

"Well, this should be interesting," he said.
Diane was mortified. "What shall I do? Do you need help - no, surely not. Oh my word!"

"Just make sure nobody comes in," Tony replied, "I'll find a way." Diane went and stood with her foot against the door, glancing back every few seconds to see how he was getting on. It was certainly complicated, but eventually the business was done. Who'd have thought that having a wee could be so tricky.

"Hope I don't need a number two!" Tony proclaimed, and they both giggled. It felt nice giggling, like the weight had shifted ever so slightly.

The doctor arrived at about 3am.

"About bloody time!" thought Diane. Tony just looked relieved. After recounting the events of the last few days for about the fifth time today, the doctor announced that he would arrange for a chest x-ray to be done.

"Hallelujah!" exclaimed Diane, when he'd left the room, "They should have done that about six hours ago." A few moments later, the doctor returned and wheeled Tony away, and Diane was left alone with her thoughts again.

Before she could begin to dwell on them though, a woman caught her eye. She was dressed in a hospital gown and was drifting along the corridor uncertainly. As she passed the door of the room it became apparent that the gown was 'all' she was wearing and she turned to go into the bathroom with her backside on display to everyone.

Diane gasped and then laughed out loud. She then felt guilty for laughing, emotions tumbling around her head and tears streaming down her face. "Unbelievable!" She muttered to herself, "pull yourself together woman."

On their return, the doctor announced that Tony's cold which had become a chest infection, had now become pneumonia, and that they would be starting him on a double-barrel course of antibiotics immediately, one intravenously and one by mouth. Tony was clearly alarmed and just nodded as the doctor showed him the x-ray and explained the plan.
"At least there's a plan now love," Diane said gently, "it's a step in the right direction."
Tony just closed his eyes and nodded.

At that moment, the most terrible hullabaloo began as a woman in a hospital gown took off at speed and raced, shrieking down the corridor, closely followed by a couple of police officers and some porters.
"What a little rascal!" remarked a nurse, as though this was an everyday occurrence.
"Well, it woke us all up, didn't it." replied her colleague, and they both laughed as the escapee was brought, wailing, back up the corridor by the two officers.
"This is a bloody madhouse!" Diane said, almost to

herself.

"Well, it's entertaining, if nothing else," said Tony, "but I could do with a bit less entertainment and a bit of shut-eye."

Antibiotics were administered and it did quieten down for a few hours, allowing Tony to doze. Diane sat back against the wall again and closed her eyes, listening to the beep-beep of the machines and the gentle snores coming from her beloved, sleeping, Tony. Whatever would she do if anything happened to him?

Determinedly, she put that thought out of her head. He was being cared for by the greatest institution in the world, the NHS, and by all these amazing people who, despite working in a total madhouse 'and' having to put up with people like her constantly asking stupid questions, came to work with a smile on their face, day-in-day-out, and saved lives.

This army of angels carried out their mysterious chaotic dance every day, and that dance would work its magic on her Tony...she just knew it!

Hide and Seek

I thought I saw the sun today
A tiny glimpse, a solitary ray.
A silvery glimmer upon the pond
A twinkle through the bracken fronds

A lighter green in the valley below
A sheen on the branch that comes and goes
The brightening promise beyond the cloud
Elusive and shifting, a heavenly shroud

A shimmer and ripple that tantalises
Then disappears as the water rises
A solitary leaf that catches the light
The summer hiding in plain sight

The glint and glitter through skeleton trees
Then carried away on the winter breeze
A rabbit's tail disappearing from view
Gracing the eye with a whiter hue

I think I saw the sun today
A chink in the armour of winter's grey
A ray of hope, maybe nature's way,
Of reminding us all that winter won't stay

May Day

Ne'er speak the names of the faerie folk
who bide 'neath the hawthorn tree
For fear their benevolent ways may turn
and their mischief be focused on thee

Just walk-on-by midst the heady scent
of the honeyed-almond blooms
Enjoy the first day of a brand-new May
Pay no heed to the fae-folks' green-rooms

Dance the 'sun-up' at dawn, on a brand-new morn'
Gather branches of green, and wildflowers
Hang the thorn tree with rushlights, with ribbons and shells
And assemble the bonfire towers

A procession to follow, to crown a May Queen
With a Maypole and feastings of quail
Jack-in-Green with a flautist and fiddler at heel
Heeds the dairymaid's' flower-filled pail

Leave a basket of treats on your neighbour's front step
Hearts of roses, or rice, for a lover
Tempt your sweetheart to kiss 'neath the apple or cherry
So they'll never leave you for another

Drive out spirits with incense on Juniper mist
In a night-time of Licentious spree
Church bells ring, bang the pots, crack the whip, raise the roof
Seven times round the house sets you free

As I Walk

Go wash your face in the morning dew
and drink spring-water on stomach empty
Make the cow jump a fire, collect pennies for may-dolls,
Drink fresh-brewed iced mug wort a-plenty

Carry bundles of wheat to Floralia's shrine
Loose a goat, free a hare to the wild
Douse the fire then re-light from the Beltaine Bonfires
To invite a new year undefiled

No, don't speak the names of the faerie folk
Let them be, in their gentle trees
Be content with the butterflies dancing on teasel
And the dandelion clocks taking flight on the breeze

A Dandy Adventure

Its 6am and the sun is just rising
A peachy hue on the distant horizon
I raise my head, then stretch out and blink
Yes, today will be the big day, I think

The clouds are gathering, soft and grey
It's going to be a breezy day
At 7am, I feel the tug
Lifted high in the air by the west wind's hug

Before I know it, I'm torn apart
My kin cast off for their own new start
Below in the field, yellow heads bob goodbye
It's 8am, and away I fly

In front of my eyes, the world unravels
This is the start of my glorious travels
Over patchwork fields and rolling hills
By 10am, village farmyards and mills

My heart is light and my mind is free
I don't see the blackbird approaching me
Like an athlete, I spin, just avoiding his beak
Emerging less bold and a little more meek

At 11 o'clock I enter the woods
To a blanket of green, full of blossoming buds
The squirrels are foraging nuts for their supper
Whilst the stream babbles on with a splash and a splutter

As I Walk

By noon I've arrived at a '*lovely*' new place
And I perch on its rushes to gaze at my face
A perfect reflection, not even a ripple
So enchanted am I, that I doze - just a little

One o'clock, two o'clock, three o'clock, four
I've seen horses in paddocks and hares on the moor
Watched new-born lambs frolic in meadows so green
And avoided an owl who looked hungry and mean

Followed people on pathways, on tracks and on lanes
All enjoying the warmth of this lovely spring day
Observed from on high, cars and buses and bikes
And passed walkers on mountain tracks, out for a hike

Five o'clock, six o'clock, time's passing fast
I'm not sure how much longer my journey can last
I long for the meadow where I left all my friends
And wonder when this big adventure will end

The breeze has now lulled as it starts to go dark
I'm floating down gently on the song of the larks
When all of a sudden, I start to feel mellow,
As I view bobbing heads - a familiar yellow

A new field, a new place, to put down some roots
Away from car tyres and big hiking boots
To sleep the big sleep through the cold winter chill
On this cosy embankment at the foot of the hill

As I Walk

It's seven o'clock, time for bed, and to rest
So that next year, my seedlings will be at their best
On the westerly wind, from this field, they'll be blown
To make Dandy Adventures and lives of their own

Mayflower Whiteout

Bourne in mid-May, it's almondy scent
Ushers joy and ambition in silent consent
A blanket of white as far as the eye
As Hawthorn dominates, field to sky

With Bitter-Cress crouching, below at its hem
Four flowers of white on a fragile stem
It hides in the shade, whilst the Mayflower shouts
"*Look around, look at me! Can there be any doubt?*"

Jack-by-the-Hedge, his white flowers in clusters
Heart-shaped leaves give aromas of mustard
Demands our attention, verdant and bright
But Mayflower's winning the battle of white

Cow Parsley offers its pretty face,
Its frothy white flowers draw pictures of lace
They bob almost regally, sway with the breeze
Seducing your eye with desire to please

"*But hark at me, my Mayflower blooms!*
My snowy white clusters, frangipane perfume
A heady exhibit for eyes and for nose
Don't let others distract from my tranquil repose"

But night-scent of campion challenges close
And tall Ox-eye Daisies do boldly boast
Wild Garlic creates an impressive crown
Its stellar white bundles make others bow down

As I Walk

Marsh Stitchwort, tiny, but so full of grace
Whilst Snow-in-Summer, our stone walls embrace
Its silvery, clinging, betangled grey down
Endeavours to steal the superb Hawthorn's crown

Yet, as sure as they try, they inevitably fail
Exquisite Mayflower ordained to prevail
Immersing us in its ethereal veil
Its seductive aroma on countryside trail

Ancient lore tells us all of the Hawthorn's intention
It's powers of healing, divine intervention
To announce spring's fertility, a brand-new beginning
Weaving peace in your mind; creativity brimming

Ahead, all I see is a blanket of white
To ease in days of summer, erase winter's blight
And whilst butterflies woo any flower in spring
The abundance of Hawthorn, in May, makes it king

It's beginning to look a lot like Springtime

If you recognize the tune, sing along.

It's beginning to look a lot like springtime
Everywhere you go
Take a look at the flowerbeds, snowdrops nodding their pearly heads
With daffodils and crocus' swaying to and fro

It's beginning to look a lot like springtime
Tulips pushing through
But the prettiest sight to see
is the sunshine through the trees
From your own front door

A flurry of starlings and song thrush that sings
to delight us ordinary folk
A robin that chirps and a wagtail that twerks
to bring us reverent hope
And Mum and Dad and kids alike can't wait to get outside

It's beginning to look a lot like springtime
Everywhere you go
There are clouds in a clear blue sky,
the kind that are white and high
The fluffy kind that never threaten pouring rain

It's beginning to look a lot like springtime
The breeze is light and warm
And the lambs as they chase and leap, will disperse your

As I Walk

winter's sleep, on your morning walk

It's beginning to look a lot like springtime
Colourful and bright
But the prettiest sight to see is sunshine through the trees
From your own front door
Sure, it's springtime ... once more

Spring is Here

April's here, the church bells ring
Bees are buzzing and the songbirds sing
The world is coming into flower
Brighter and bolder by the hour
Children play and new lambs scamper
Whilst mums prepare the Easter hamper
Chocolate eggs and hot cross buns
Let's thank the Lord that spring has come

Camino

Follow the arrows, uphill and down
The bright yellow arrows that lead out of town
They're painted on street signs, on walls and on posts
And wherever they're pointing - that's where you go

Walking on pavements and old cobbled streets
Through the old city town where Oporto's heart beats
Quaint Quinta's replaced by a great city sprawl
Where instead of bright tiles, there's graffiti on walls

Follow the arrows along roads and tracks
With feet that are aching and heavy backpacks.
The sprawl becomes suburbs, then villages and trees
The sun beating down through a gentle breeze

So follow the arrows, let your feet lead the way
Hour after hour, and day after day
Forget all the troubles that live in your head
Just enjoy the walk, the good food and your bed.

Found

As the crack of light widened, my heart raced. At last, the possibility of one last performance.

I had lain here since 1974, fifty years gathering dust and losing hope, but now there was a chance I would sing again.

A hand reached down from the brightness above, lifting me slowly, carefully, and eventually blowing off the dust to gasp aloud.

"I've found it!" A voice exclaimed.

I was lowered gently onto the turntable, a stylus placed at my outer groove, and once more my voice was released, rising into the room to rapturous applause.

It was worth the wait.

Serendipity

A pool day beckons
A blue sky without blemish
Scorching amber sun

Whisper of a breeze
It's touch caressing hot skin
Like a lover's kiss

Olive trees stand guard
Providing shade from their boughs
Ancient and knowing

The pool, deep, cooling
An escape from the day's heat
Drawing me under

Then repeat - sun, shade, pool
blissful in its simple form
Serendipity

The Gift of a Breeze

The summer winds, they bode no ill
They bring no cold your bones to chill
A gentle breeze, a warm caress
The briefest breath, a welcome guest

A playful hand running through your hair
To make you feel without a care
A rippling, tickling, fleeting touch
There to feel but leaves no smutch

It's warm, yet cooling, on your skin
A soft embrace to sink therein
But after the dip of the late summer sun
You may well think the breeze has gone

A chill arrives to take its place
To whip your hair and slap your face
To bend the boughs and churn the seas
As wild, as gentle is the breeze

But as sure as Earth is slowly turning
Next year the breeze will be returning
For summer winds they bode no ill
They bring just warmth your heart to fill

Slow-Walking

At the pace of a child the world slows down
There's no place for worries or even a frown
Just the joy of discovery, wonder and awe
That are lost as we grow to accept the world's flaws
Flaws brought about by our cold human touch
As we side with the monsters and the power they clutch

In the eyes of a child every day is a picture
Every animal, flower and tree makes them richer
A bumble bee searching, a heron in flight
Wild flowers that dance in the morning sunlight
They walk slowly to make sure they don't miss a thing
And absorb all the beauty our great planet brings

With the ears of a child there is no time for thought
Or for chatter or music - just the sounds they have caught
The babble of water that winds through the moss
The low of the cow and the neigh of the horse
The cry of a seagull, the chirp of the cricket
Raindrops on sycamore and a rustle in the thicket

If we all could hold on to the wonder of children
Accepting and loving this world we've been given
We'd walk a bit slower, and look a bit harder
To see, hear and treasure, it's art, song and larder
And people in power could learn from the children
If they did some 'slow-walking' in our garden of Eden

Betwixt

Early September is sent to confuse us
Her split personality will often bemuse us
Neither autumn nor summer, our mind's in a fix
Not one or the other, but somewhere betwixt

If you put on your coat there will surely be sun
But with sunglasses on you can guarantee none
In a t-shirt you're chilled, in a jacket you'll swelter
You're riding the seasonal helter-skelter

The days can be warm, reminiscent of summer
But when we reach sundown the mercury plummets
Is it time for the fire? No! Surely not yet
So, on go the jumpers, the bed socks and vests

Although there seems to be no rhyme or reason
'Tis clear there's a stand-off between the seasons
Summer's not gone yet, but autumn awaits
To make her bold entrance and put forth her case.

September evenings are drawing in
And autumn will certainly, this battle, win
Mother nature moves on, her actions are zealous
Replacing the greens with reds, browns and yellows

As I Walk

The summer days have faded now
The breeze is cooler on my brow
But when I look at autumn's treasure
I give thanks for each in equal measure
Neither autumn or summer, but a perfect mix
Not one or the other just somewhere betwixt

If

If I were a little girl again,
I'd go to the Billy Goats bridge.
I'd peep underneath at the ugly old troll,
then tiptoe across like a thief.

If I saw a black sheep amongst all the white,
I'd ask, 'Where did your woolly coat go?
Did you give it the little girl, master or dame?
Won't you miss it when winter brings snow?'

I'd talk to the dicky birds sat on the wall
and say to them, 'Please won't you stay?
I'm desperate to meet you and know your 'real' names
But you always fly off, far away.'

I'd find Mother Hubbard sat by her bare cupboard
And tell her, 'Go out for a stroll.
You'll find mushrooms and berries, and apples so sweet,
then you wouldn't be hungry at all.'

I would watch the Pied Piper across the high field,
with his two trusty pals Meg and Bess.
With a yell and a whistle, the flock's moved along,
with the sheep looking less than impressed.

I would play hide and seek with the squirrels and mice
among tree stumps, gorse bushes and trees.
I would lie in the meadow and soak up the sun,
and find pictures in clouds on the breeze.

As I Walk

If I were a little girl again
I'd seek magical creatures and places.
Then I'd write my own stories for children to read,
and enjoy the delight on their faces.

September Rain

September rain.

A storm; stair-rods hurtling downwards like glass spears.

Piercing the canopy at will, all life darting for cover.

Disintegrating. A billion tiny crystals as they hit the ground and vanish.

Gentler now, its temper spent.

A lullaby of pitter-patter on the leaves above.

An apology.

Autumn is Here

There is no denying that autumn is here
Despite the birdsong gracing my ear
Despite the soft touch of the rippling breeze and the warmth
of the sun as it peeps through the trees

The cows are still grazing and the sky remains blue
But autumn is here, I can feel it, can't you?
It's here in the leaves that are changing their hues
In the harvested fields - and there are other clues:

The lambs are now wearing their wintery coats
There are acorns and berries and conkers to tote
The stream's flowing faster, the squirrels are hoarding
Yes, autumn is here and the landscape's transforming

When life gets messy

When we are tangled up in the complicated patterns of life, it is sometimes hard to do know what to do for the best, and even harder to explain our actions to our nearest and dearest.

Harry jolted awake as the front door slammed.

Jenny looked flustered as she deposited a cardboard coffee cup on the table and shrugged off her coat.

"Sorry I'm late Grandad, it's carnage out there."

"Well you shouldn't have left it 'till rush hour"

"I know, I know, but ... I had a client and it ran over."

Jenny popped back in and scooped up the ready meal. Hotpot. He preferred the lasagne.

"No lasagne today Gramps, sorry, this was all they had."

He grunted and stared at the coffee cup. Why didn't she just buy a jar of instant? She was always claiming to be skint and what those coffee shops were charging was daylight robbery.

"You should have just bought a jar, it's cheaper." he said, pointing at the coffee.

"Ah well, it's a little treat isn't it, Double Caramel Mocha."

She put the plastic tray of food down in front of him. He preferred it on a plate but he better not say anything. He started to eat, chewing slowly, his dentures finding a piece of gristle amongst the veg and gravy. He spat it out and pointedly wrapped it in a tissue before holding it out to her.

Without comment, she took it from him and dropped it in the kitchen bin, before settling herself in the armchair opposite, a bottle of plain water in hand. That was probably from the coffee shop as well. Couldn't she turn on a tap?

"Well Grandad, have you had a nice day?"

He frowned at her over his glasses and carried on eating.

"I've been run off my feet; two bikini waxes, an eyebrow re-shape and three foot massages. Oh, and a facial skin peel."

"Why don't you get a proper job instead of pandering to people's expensive and unnecessary needs?" he pronounced; a rhetorical question that he regularly repeated.

"Never mind that, have you thought about what we talked about yesterday?

"What you talked about, you mean."

Jenny sighed. "You can't stay here much longer Gramps, you can't manage by yourself. You need looking after now that Gran's gone."

"I've got you haven't I?" Another rhetorical question.

They both sat in silence for a few moments before Jenny spoke up again.

"You do know you'll lose the house if you have to go into care?"

Harry rose to his feet unsteadily. "I've told you, you can have my house when I'm dead!" he barked. "Now, if you don't mind, I'm going for a lie down."

He left the room, leaning heavily on his stick and muttering under his breath.

Jenny cleared away his tea tray, washed the dishes that had been left in the sink and half-filled the kettle for his bedtime hot chocolate, before peeping in at his bedroom door.

"See you tomorrow then, call if you need me."

He replied with a wave of his hand, almost a dismissal, and she bit her tongue as she left, resisting the urge to slam the front door behind her.

Jenny climbed into her old Ford Escort and sat for a moment, tears stinging her eyes. She had been caring for her Grandad for five years now, since Gran died, and it wasn't getting any easier.

She had been talking to a client a couple of weeks ago who had told her that she had signed over her whole life to her son: signed over the deeds to her house and given him power of attorney so that she wouldn't have to spend her whole worth on care home fees when the time came. She planned to spend all of her money having a great time until she was "*decrepit* or *doo-lally*" - her words.

Jenny was horrified. "But where are you living?"

"Oh, I get to stay in my house, they just can't take it off me to pay for care, and when I do pop-me-clogs, its already his. No fuss about inheritance."

She had told her grandad about the woman, explaining as best she could and hoping he would think about it. After all, he had told her often enough that the house was hers when he went, and it would simplify matters. His response had been the same as today, "You can have my house when I'm dead." She had been quite offended, she wasn't after his money, she was just trying to be pragmatic.

Jenny should have led a different life. Her grandad was right about her job; it was rubbish pay and she spent her days pandering to the whims of rich ladies and daft girls. She had been all set to go to university. She got great A-level grades and had been accepted at Lancaster to study business; far enough to have to live away, but close enough to pop home whenever she wanted to.

But then her gran died quite suddenly. Jenny had lost her mum when she was quite young; her dad had never been on the scene and she had spent ten years living with her grandparents whom she loved dearly.

Overnight, her life and her plans changed. She couldn't leave her grandad on his own, so she got an apprenticeship at a local salon and moved into a tiny flat above a smelly kebab shop on the high street. She worked hard all day and then every evening, after work, she called in at her grandad's with his supper and his favourite 'expensive' coffee - the one he had always ordered when he treated her and gran to coffee and a slice of lemon drizzle on a Sunday afternoon.

He hadn't always been a grumpy old man and he had always been there for her, so she was devastated that he now seemed to think she was after his money; she wished she had never mentioned it.

Harry lay for a long time with his eyes closed. Jenny was right, he needed to sort things out why he still could. The problem was that it wasn't as simple as just signing over the house. If it was, he would do it in a heartbeat; there was no house to sign over - there was nothing.

When Mary had become ill, a lot earlier than Jenny was aware of, they had put the house into a shared ownership scheme; handing over their home to a company who then allowed them to live there as long as they needed to. This had freed up a bit of cash so that they could enjoy a few holidays while she was still able, and put a bit aside should Jenny want to go to university or buy her own place. He had paid the deposit on her little flat and helped her to kit it out, the plan being that when she went to uni she could rent it out to help ends meet.

When Mary's health had taken a sudden downturn, it had taken them all by surprise. He really hadn't wanted Jenny to change her plans, but she had refused to move away, instead taking that ridiculous job painting nails.

And now he was stuck. Jenny wasn't being callous, she was being sensible. How was he going to explain this whole mess.

The next afternoon, Jenny made sure that she was early. She also made sure that she had bought Grandads favourite lasagne - for two.

When she walked in, she noticed that he had tidied up a bit, and that there was a pile of envelopes on the sideboard.

"Hi Gramps, lasagne tonight...and I picked up a lemon drizzle cake for us, a little treat."

It was Harry's turn to feel the tears pricking at his eyes, and he wiped them away quickly as she went into the kitchen to heat up the lasagne and put the kettle on.

"Sit down love, we need to talk."

By the time he had finished they were both in tears.

"Oh, Grandad, why didn't you tell me all this earlier?"

"I'd always promised you the house... and now I've nothing for you. I didn't know how."

His voice trailed off and he stared out of the window, somehow a shrunken version of the man he had been an hour earlier.

"Get your coat on," she said, "We're going out."

They sat in companionable silence, two extra-large double caramel mochas and a large slice of lemon drizzle cake on the table in front of them.

"It'll be Ok Gramps. We've got each other, you have a roof over your head for as long as you need it, and I have my whole life ahead of me to go to uni' and get a better job."

"I don't deserve you." Harry said, grasping her hand. "I don't deserve you, but I'm glad I've got you. Let's have another coffee."

Colours of Autumn

Bright holly berries and maple leaves
Squirrels collecting their nuts and seeds
Rosy cheeks on a frosty day
As children wrap up warm to play

Orange leaves of the sturdy oak
Toasty soldiers in a runny yolk
The toothy grin of a pumpkin ghoul
And glowing embers as the bonfire cools

The yellowing fall of the sycamore tree
The last of the wasp and the bumble bee
The weakening sun as it slips from the sky
As the moon takes its place to watch from on high

The ivy, a home for the birds and the bugs
Thick chicken soup in oversized mugs
The grass remains green but enters its slumber
Whilst the fir trees stand guard over all lying under

There's an icy blue to the autumn sky
And the stream is now hurried as it rushes on by
Fires are lit and we turn back the clocks
Yet violas and pansies stand proud in their pots

As the fern turns to bracken all crispy and brown
The acorns and chestnuts all fall to the ground
And whilst stars prick their holes in an inky black sky
The first frost of autumn waves summer goodbye

The Nothing Day

Half-light, half-bright
Not quite morning, neither night
The breeze is still, the birds are quiet
A nothing day, an empty riot

The oak stands tall, it's mood contrite
A Robin lands but then takes flight
The earth accepts its solemn plight
A nothing day, the image trite

The fox skulks on, its tail tucked tight
A russet blur and flash of white
The verdict brought, a bleak indict
A nothing day, a sickly blight

Half-light, half-bright
Not quite evening, not yet night
It's almost gone, this mild affray
Tomorrow's memory, a nothing day.

November's Nuance

November's nuance
Neither summer nor winter
Its weather makes for a fickle friend
A glimpse of sun at the rainbow's end
A chill in the air

Arise to sunshine
Glinting temptation through curtains
But before breakfast is hurriedly taken,
a torrent of rain pelting and breaking
the stems of summer blooms

Brushing fallen leaves
raises the wrath of the autumn wind
Tearing through oak and sycamore
Their autumn foliage left on the floor,
branches bare

And then a cruel reminder:
Breeze dropped, clouds banished, a blue sky
A milky sun brings a warm caress;
a brief interlude, the balance redressed
November's nuance

A Prayer

I have lain for hours.
Not asleep;
a knotted ball of misery
sits heavy in my heart.
I wish I could dream,
light and free.
Released from the malignant thoughts
of this cruel helplessness.

I would change places
in a heartbeat,
to know what you are feeling.
A chance, at least, to help.
Just to bring you peace;
to release you
from the war that rages on,
tormenting your soul!

I yearn for days gone.
Simple days
where pleasure was just being;
did not need to be sought.
I '*am*' grateful for what we have had
but it's not enough!
I want more, of you, of us,
our easy companionship.

As I Walk

I pray for a future -
not too distant.
When we will rise again together:
Joined in our love, at peace, strong.

The Old Oak

You seem barely alive with your hollowed out trunk
You can't stand up straight, are diminished and shrunk
Anorexic branches, blackened and gnarled
Twisted and reaching like the arms of a child
Unadorned for so long, you seem withered and torn
Your all-seeing eyes view new saplings with scorn
As your roots reach and feel for a foothold below
You lament what has gone but are desperate to grow

You seem barely alive, but you have a strong heart
Just awaiting the springtime for life to restart

Nature's Rainbow

Spring green
Sky blue
Primrose yellow
Nature's hue

Blossom pink
Sparrow brown
Iris purple
Nature's crown

Hawthorn white
Heron grey
Poppy's scarlet
Nature's day

Silver droplets
fall from high
Natures rainbow
fills the sky

The School Run

Out of bed and into the shower
Ablutions done, we've got an hour!
Husbands gone - this week on earlies
Wake the boy and then the girlies

Get them washed and get them dressed
Clothes all ready, uniforms pressed
Down for breakfast round the table
Eat and chat, TV disabled

Eggs or cereal, toast and tea
Debate at length but won't agree
Upstairs, clean teeth, find shoes and bags
They dilly-dally, mother nags

PE kit, homework, reading books
The littlest wants his favourite truck
Coats and hats on, scarves and gloves
And out the door with push and shoves

Into car and seat belts on,
Luggage loaded, time is gone
Arrive, spill out, we're just in time
A kiss, a wave, it's five to nine

Back in the car, the school run done
Her own day's work must be begun
A job to do, a role to play
Before another ground-hog day

Tick Tock

We are not always in control of our lives and their events, but often it is the choices that we do make that can be the difference between success and failure, happiness and sadness, even life and death.

I opened my eyes. Slowly, millimetre by millimetre, until I could see a smudge of blue sky through the dusty haze; a soupy mist which seemed to float towards me and yet linger afar; near, yet distant.

I could hear nothing. Neither did I have the ability (or was it the will?) to move.

I felt as though I was suspended in a silent cerulean pool; womb-like, comforting, other-worldly.

Maybe I was dreaming. Is that a thought you would have whilst asleep?

Could this be heaven... or hell? That would mean that I was dead. Strangely, the possibility did not disturb me: no panic, no regret, no... anything.

I closed my eyes, totally at peace, accepting of whatever this moment meant.

I opened my eyes again, but this time there was nothing. Blackness. Absence.

Now the panic began to stir; to rise like a snake uncoiling in the pit of my stomach. Now I *did* want to move - but still I couldn't. I felt leaden, as though buried alive. As though pinned down by an unseen and malevolent force.

I could feel heat, maybe through exertion, maybe through climate, possibly fire - I couldn't tell.

Despite the absence of sight, I squeezed my eyes shut as the snake moved faster, racing towards my throat.

The pain invaded every inch of my being as I vomited, my body lurching and heaving as I began to choke. The snake was expelled, but the dread, the horror and torment remained, intensified.
I was engulfed by an ocean of blackness and the last thing I was aware of was the pain; it consumed me.
If this was death, I welcomed it.

"Tick, tock, tick tock"
... not a clock, a voice. A woman's voice.
My eyes snapped open. A room. A dirty box, eight by eight if that. Dusty boxes with strange script on the sides of each one. The same phrase over and over, but not one I could read. Pictures. Guns.
"Tick tock, tick tock"
I tried to scream before the darkness returned.

So, I'm not dead... and I'm not blind. Hope surged through me for the first time.
My thoughts raced as I recalled my last awakening. How long were these periods of unconsciousness? Was I sleeping or was I being drugged. What the hell was going on? Where was I? Who was I?
I certainly seemed more lucid now and strained to remember. I opened my eyes - just a slit - just enough to see the boxes, the dirty walls, a shadow.
I could hear crying. A baby's wail. Not hungry or demanding, but resigned, desperate, as though even the infant knew there was no hope - yet still dared to try.
My niece, my sister's daughter, came to mind. Her face was contorted, her mouth an angry, empty 'o', her eyes screwed up and her skin puce as she bellowed her furious demands to whoever would listen. That was the face of a baby whose

As I Walk

mother would come running. That noise had purpose.
I haven't seen my sister in a long time, her daughter never, I wonder why?
Silent tears streamed down my face uncontrollably. I couldn't escape the sadness - was drowning in it.

The ache pervaded every part of me. My head was the worst, it was as though bombs were exploding, shrapnel lodging itself deep in my brain, a hammer banging it home. Grenades were exploding, and then the world went quiet - an unearthly stillness that was somehow worse - before the screaming began.
Voices.
Shouting.
Running.

The room is now devoid of boxes.
No shadow.
But no panic either, just that lazy river of thought - an apple tree, a pretty girl - older than me - is it my mother? A picnic. Sleep.

The eyes that I wake to are cold; beautiful, but cold. They just stare at me without emotion. She turns and walks away.
A person. The first I have seen in... I don't know how long. How long have I been here? Was hers the face of the shadow? Why does she not speak?

I rubbed my eye and winced. I *rubbed my eye*! I raised a hand slowly. Blood, dirt, I could not tell the colour of my skin. Tentatively, I moved the rest: my legs, shoulders, head, arms... my arm. I couldn't move my left arm!

I turned my head and screamed. A bandaged stump emerged from the standard army commission sleeve, bloodied and dirty.

Fury flooded through my veins and I riled against the ropes, the restraints, despite the agony brought on by the sudden movement. It was every soldier's nightmare, to be taken hostage, tortured. Being killed was not the worst thing that could happen to you. Was I a soldier?

I remember walking through woodland with my father, dust motes twinkling through sunlight. We were stalking.

"Shh!"

My father crept ahead and I watched; watched in awe as he raised his gun noiselessly and pulled the trigger. The deer dropped and writhed in agony - it was not a clean kill.

A few years earlier, I would have been horrified - disgusted by this pointless and inhumane action.

My father slapped me on the back as we high-fived, grins as wide as our faces.

"Your turn kid. Kill or be killed.'

I took my turn.

Over and over, I took my turn. Kill or be killed.

"Tick tock, tick tock."

This time I didn't open my eyes. I was upright, my chin lolling on my chest. My brain was racing. Think! Think!

The breath left my body as a fist of iron met my abdomen. I jerked backwards, gasping but alert, eyes now wide to take in the scene.

I was on a chair, still bound and gagged.

A man looked on with hooded eyes that did nothing to hide

his anger - his hatred.

"Are you feeling better?"

Still reeling, I turned my head towards the voice. Her face was covered, but... those eyes!

"I was!"

She spoke in broken English, quietly and calmly. "They left you for dead, your comrades. We have been tending you for two weeks. You almost didn't make it, which would have been a shame."

I was filled with gratitude - and with the image of a woman and child.

"The baby?" I questioned.

"Is fine," She replied. "No thanks to you."

My blood ran cold as the scene unfolded in my memory for the first time. A woman and child. A garden. A picnic. The woman saw me and smiled as she reached into the picnic basket.

I lifted my rifle.

It was a clean shot.

I needed you recovered. My father has lost a daughter, my niece her mother. I needed you to know that before..."

She paused for the longest moment.

"...Tick tock, tick tock."

My insides turned to liquid as she raised the gun. I closed my eyes and waited, resigned to my fate – one clean shot.

Seconds passed.

"I am not like you," she said, revulsion evident in her tone. "You will live, thanks to me, and I will return you to where we found you. Maybe your colleagues will return for you, but I doubt it. You are in control of your own future. It is up to you to make the right choices from now on. Make your life count, you only have one shot at it."

Just one shot, 'Tick Tock'.

The Shroud

The ethereal cloak of a misty morn
It's cutting chill like daggers drawn
The day to come, beyond the dawn,
is hidden 'neath the gloom

The air sits silent, feels the threat
Of the damp and shifting faery net
Occluding thought as minds are met
Lest optimism blooms

The breeze laid low, its breath is still
The only sound the old church bell
Which peals a question, "Heaven or hell?"
You choose the daily tune

But then a glimpse, a muted glow
The shroud retreats its heavenly show
To lick its wounds and so lay low
Thus light has ousted gloom

So use your spells your chants your wit
For sadness is a lousy fit
It creeps and claws and seeps and picks
If you allow it room

Yet once released from darkened clouds
Your message will be clear and loud
To banish such unwanted shrouds
And send them to their doom

As I Walk

For like your strength, your mood will lift
And far away that shroud will drift
To be replaced by welcome gifts
Of peace and fortitude

When Life Gives Me Lemons

I like that the wind can hurl me its bluster, but not knock me down
I like that the clouds can throw me their tears, but not make me cry
I like that the hail can pelt her tiny marbles, but that I can turn my back and laugh
I like that the mist can surround me in its veil, but not get me lost
I like that the sun can scorch my skin, but another will grow
I like that the frost can nip at my fingers, but not to the bone
I like that the ice can cover my path, but not take my balance
I like that I am better than those things, that I can outsmart them, my wit a shield to their evil charms
When the world gives me weather and that weather is unkind, I like that I can write a poem and hurl it straight back
I like that.

As I Walk

Hamstrung in December

It started in September, this niggly leg,
not hugely surprising, considering our trek.
First Prague then Vienna, Bratislava came next,
Budapest then Lisbon then Funchal for a rest.
Five cities, four countries what sights and what smiles;
Our feet walked one hundred and fifty odd miles

Back home in October, the leg niggled more,
it ached when I sat, became troublesome and sore.
My response was to go out and walk myself stronger,
my leg must be weak so my walks should be longer.
Up hills and down valleys, through woods, grass and hay;
it didn't hurt when I walked, so I walked every day.

It didn't get worse, but it didn't get better
and I worked in November teaching numbers and letters.
Standing up, sitting down, every morning and then
a walk after lunch in the fresh air again.
Until one afternoon, at the end of November,
a sudden sharp pain I will always remember.

Now it hurt when I walked, when I sat, when I lay,
and the horrible ache just would not go away.
Dr Google informed me that my hamstring was torn
- or pulled, or strained - I was very forlorn.
Because worse than the pain, and this made me baulk,
the only way forward was to rest, so no walks!

Hamstrung in December with nothing to do,
just sat on the sofa with a book and a brew.

As I Walk

I could play my guitar, play a game on my phone,
watch a film, try to enjoy some 'me' time, alone.
Half hourly compresses, first cold and then hot,
with a minimal step count, frustrated a lot!

But I had learned a lesson, so I did as was told
remaining sedentary, letting two weeks unfold.
And when I felt better, my leg feeling mended,
the muscle well rested, my hamstring well-tended,
I eased myself back into backpack and boots
and prepared for adventure on my easier routes.

Now feeling much better and back on the trails,
exploring new places with the wind in my sails
enjoying the freedom and joy my walks bring,
the babble of brooks and the songbirds that sing.
But not pushing too hard for I will always remember,
It was horrible being hamstrung in December.

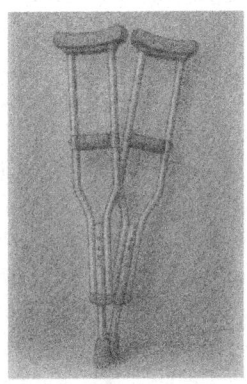

Snow Days

For a child, a snowy winter's day
brings great delight and the promise of play
To open the curtains to a blanket of white
is always a thrilling and beautiful sight
The crunch that is made by wellington boots
As snug as a bug in a scarf and snow-suit
Slipping and sliding on the walk up to school
And then after, the snowball fights, all in, no rules
When mittens are sodden and fingers are frozen
back home for hot chocolate to thaw out cold noses

Once grown, there remains the excitement and thrill
But also concerns about ice and the chill
There are paths that need gritting and black ice on roads
and journeys to work in the ice and the snow
Elderly people to keep safe and warm
and children to watch as they play and have fun
Store cupboards to fill just in case you're snowed in
and fuel to buy to fill up the coal bin

With wood to collect and bird feeders to fill
We sometimes forget just to stop and be still
The feeling's still there on that cold icy morning
When the world is a Christmas card, frost is adorning
The hillsides are glistening with a dusting of white
And the trees are all frozen, bark sparkling bright
As I walk down the lane there's a satisfying crunch
And the robins are searching for grubs for their lunch

See the glint of the sun in the late afternoon
As it casts its long shadows, making way for the moon
Freezing fog hangs in valleys as day turns to night,
For the beauty of winter is a breath-taking sight

A Child's Voice

"What would you like for Christmas this year?" The
gentleman asked the child.
He watched as the child's eyes lit up, just for a moment,
before dulling at the memory of his reality.
The child spoke, carefully, for this was important.

"For safety," he said with certainty.
"For a home I can be sure I will be returning to.
For a bed of our own, my brother and I;
For quiet, all through the night."

He thought again.
"That my father will return and my mother stop crying.
That there will be enough food and clean water.
That the fighting will stop."

"I miss my school, my friends, the books.
New things for my mind to wonder at.
Knowledge of a world where things can be different,
where we are all accepted."

The man asked, "What about gifts? A new toy, clothes?"
The boy was incredulous, unbelieving of the man's naivety.

"What is the point of new shoes when there is nowhere to
walk in safety?
Who would play with a toy when there is no playfulness in
their heart?
What good are things when there is fear and hunger?"

The man looked at the boy, wise beyond his years.
"What you say is true, but you must always have hope.
There may not be a way for you, but you can be the difference, the way forward, to forge a better future for your people."

The boy contemplated the man's words.
"You are right. I don't know the way forward, but I will look for the path.
The future starts with me, and people like me, who will believe in a future of safety, peace and humanity.
That is what I want. Maybe not this Christmas, but one Christmas. Maybe not for me, but for the children of the future."

Winter

It's dark all day and it's dark all night
The sun comes around but the clouds hide the light
The world feels small but the sky seems huge,
pressing down on the earth with its colourless hues.

Mist, like a veil, is dropped and then lifted
Shadows unstable, reality shifted
Seamlessly, day seems to slip into night
Familiar images stolen from sight

The stars remain absent, the moon is obscured
The sunrise awaited; its promise assured
The owl and the fox fail to visit tonight,
leaving just silence, a deafening quiet

Trees stand like giants, unmoving yet bold
Without fur or feather, their story untold
A chill in the air, a traitorous tryst
As their leaves fall to ground, and lie there, dew-kissed

At dawn, the birdsong is muted and low
The blackbird and sparrow don't put on their show
Daylight unfolds as a cold, milky gloom
And lamplight is needed in every room

Dawn becomes morning, becomes afternoon,
The fire is lit and the coals warm the room
Maybe tomorrow the light will return
Until then, the bitter outdoors I will spurn

Martyr

I stood forlorn my boughs weighed heavy.
A shadow of myself, in a corner of the garden; half hidden behind the garden shed, head bowed, ashamed.
At first I had been elated at my promotion:
From pot to soil, inside to out.
No longer trivial – a plaything, dressed up by children in a gaudy sash, but free to reach up high, to feel the sun, to sink my roots into endless, soft earth; to live.

But was this living?
A fruitless existence, a friendless realm.
There was no admiration from sparrow, finch or wren; no lit-up faces, no squeals of joy.
Just tiny claws scratching, beaks pecking, grubs burying beneath my bark.
Beneath the soil, my roots assaulted by shrew and mole
Above, no star atop, just scorching sun, gusty gale or hurtling hail.

Slowly, over time, perspective was gained. Hope lost. Why go on?
Unwanted, unloved, abused and neglected.
Until one day... one frozen, sodden, miserable day, he returned.
With a spade my roots were severed, an unbearable, agonizing assault, and then nothing.
Until awoken, a welcome transformation, the better of two evils, warm and dry.

Baubles, tinsel, and a silver star returned to its rightful place.
I was reborn, loved by all, a willing martyr.

The Dance of the Sugar Plum Fairy

When you are young and pursuing your dreams, it is always good to have family on your side. Who will be there for Grace when she really needs it?

She stood at the window. This should have been the greatest moment of her young life, but all she felt was the clench of nerves in her stomach and a niggling doubt in her mind. The lady who had welcomed her had been friendly enough, and her room was lovely, but she still felt out of place. Imposter syndrome maybe, it still didn't feel real.

It was early evening and all the other students were lazing on the grass in front of the impressive old Georgian building, laughing, fooling around or reading. They all looked completely at home. Would she ever feel comfortable in her own skin?

It was not surprising that she doubted herself, for others had always doubted her too. After all, not many girls aspired to be a prima ballerina – not with any real conviction anyway. After her mum died when she was a toddler, she had gone to live with her Great Aunt Maud. She was kind enough – motherly even, but she was a lot older than the other mums at school and Grace often felt embarrassed when she was dropped off and collected, and then tortured herself with guilt for feeling embarrassed; after all, her Great Aunt had saved her from the care system and had also encouraged her to follow her dream and dance.

Encouragement was something she didn't get from

her teachers, sadly. Although they pretended to recognise her dream, they always added a pinch of sobering realism:

'You need to have a back-up plan...'

'It's a very difficult field to succeed in, maybe you could be a dance teacher.'

And one particularly unkind comment that had always plagued her, '*You're not really the right shape.*'

The tears sprung to her eyes as she recalled that moment in her young life. She was five years old for goodness' sake, and had gone home to her Great Aunt distraught. To her credit, Maud had immediately enrolled her for ballet and tap classes at the local church hall, where the lovely, kind, Miss Butterfield had nurtured her confidence and trained her wayward limbs.

Over the years she had become a competent – no, a good – dancer, and blossomed from 'good toes, naughty toes', to 'arabesques, pirouettes, grand jetés and complex enchaînements, and from leather ballet slippers to ribboned block-toed satin shoes. She worked hard, spending hours in the practice studio and surviving the excruciating transition to pointe shoes, learning to bind her bruised toes with lambs' wool and darn her blocks regularly. It was a fact that without Miss Butterfield, who allowed her to use the studio free of charge whenever there wasn't a class on, and Maud who paid for all of her lessons, shoes, leotards, tutus and examination fees, she would not be where she was today.

Grace pinched herself. It was her sixteenth birthday and here she was, a scholar at the great White Lodge, home to the younger students of the famous Royal Ballet School.

A knock at the door drew her from her reverie, and she wiped the tears from her eyes.

Before she could respond, the door was flung open and a pretty, doll-like girl breezed in, gathering her into an unexpected warm embrace.

"You're here at last! Come along, let me show you around."

The next hour was spent in a dizzying whirl of activity, as Marguerite gave Grace the grand tour. The three-hundred-year-old building was now unrecognisable as a hunting lodge, and had been repurposed and continually developed since the 1950s.

Having only ever seen White Lodge through pictures in the brochure and online, Grace was mesmerised by the myriad of rooms: classrooms, practice rooms, dance studios, dining room and recreational facilities, including a swimming pool and tennis courts. Each of the cosy common rooms was surprisingly homely, with squishy sofas, games, TV, and even video games.

But the one space that Grace had been most eager to see completely exceeded her expectations; The Fonteyn Studio Theatre, named after her heroine, Margo Fonteyn.

As they walked into the huge space, her heart soared and tears, once again pricked at her eyes – this time out of sheer joy and complete amazement. Marguerite gently propelled her forward, guiding her down the wide aisle towards the stage.

"It's beautiful," she gasped, "it's everything I

imagined and more, just stunning."

"And one day you will be up there, watched by hundreds of people, doing what you were meant to do." whispered Marguerite.

Grace spun to face her, completely overwhelmed and suddenly filled with self-doubt.

"I can't do this. I'm just a nobody. People like me don't belong here! I'm poor, and an orphan, and I'm probably not even going to be the right shape for a ballerina."

Marguerite took her by the shoulders and looked intently into her eyes. "You are in exactly the right place; you were made for this. You just need to believe in yourself."

Back in her room, Grace lay on the bed pinching herself. Was she really here? Was this really happening to her?

"Well, I suppose I had better unpack then." She said to herself, a small bubble of confidence growing inside her.

She had an hour before dinner, just one more hour before she would meet all her fellow students and become part of the White Lodge family; and just one more night before she started her lessons and set out on the path to her dream.

Slowly and methodically, she began to unpack, hanging her few clothes on the rail in the small wardrobe and packing her practise bag for the next morning. At the bottom of the bag was a parcel that she didn't remember seeing when she packed.

Curiously, she lifted it out and placed it on the desk. The parcel itself looked quite old, wrapped with old-fashioned brown paper and stuck with brittle, cracked tape which just about held it together. It was tied with string, and pushed underneath the string was a new envelope with her name written on it, just one word, Grace.

She opened the envelope and began to read. It was from her Great Aunt Maud.

Dearest Grace,

It has been a pleasure to raise you for the last twelve years, and to watch you grow into the beautiful and talented girl that you are. That does not come without hard work, though, and I could not be more proud of the way you have overcome the obstacles that life has put in your way and are now realising your dream. I cannot wait to be sat in the audience watching you shine on a stage somewhere as Odette or Giselle, or maybe even the Sugar Plum Fairy, which I know is your favourite. Whatever role you dance, I know that you will be amazing and I have no doubts that one day you will be the prima ballerina that you have always dreamed to be, and have continued to work so hard for even when people doubted you or let you down.

I never doubted you, Grace, and neither did your mother. I'm afraid I have not been entirely open with you about your mother. Yes, she was my niece, and yes, she did leave you in my care twelve years ago, but I was vague about the circumstances of her death as I didn't want to make life any more difficult than it already was for you, as an orphan. The truth is that she was quite unstable. Your father was an important man, but he was already married and when your mother found herself pregnant with you, he vanished. I don't believe she ever saw him again.

She adored you, though Grace, and always called you her little ballerina, and I know that if she were here today, she would be thrilled at your success, and so, so proud of you. So, when you get up on that stage for the first time, I will be watching from the stalls, but your mother will also be looking down on you, I promise.

The parcel you have just discovered was left for you by her and I have kept it safe for all these years not knowing what is inside; I am as intrigued as you are, believe me. She asked me to give it to you on your sixteenth birthday, which will be next week, on your first day at White Lodge. I was sorely tempted to give it to you before you left, but I felt that I had to honour her wishes, so I am left wondering. Please let me know what is inside, it must have been very important to her.

So, I leave you in the place where you belong, to fulfil your career and dreams, but be assured that as long as I live, I will always be here for you.

With love and affection, your Great Aunt Maud.

It was true, Grace had always wondered about her father and about the circumstances of her mother's death, but when she had asked Maud, she had been vague, claiming that she and her mother weren't close and that she didn't know, just telling the story of a call from a social worker asking if she would care for Grace as her next of kin and her only family member.

And that she had done, and done with love and kindness, and Grace considered herself fortunate to have been so lucky; but she had wondered about her parents; her birth certificate only recorded hers and her mother's name, the space where her father's name should have been staring at her like an open wound.

She stared at the package on the desk, wanting to open it but apprehensive about what she may find under the layers of brown paper. Slowly, she untied the string, tied in a simple bow. The first layer of paper fell away, the glue on the tape being old and no longer sticky. The second layer had held better and she picked at the ends of the tape, trying to unfasten it without ripping the paper. In the end, she had to though, and as it fell away, it revealed a small music box, made of white leather and decorated with pink roses. Grace flicked open the clasp and slowly lifted the lid, bringing to life a twirling ballerina rotating slowly to the tune of the Sugar Plum Fairy.

Inside the box was another simple white envelope, once again labelled with her name, this time in her mother's handwriting, and she held it in her hand for several long minutes before opening it and sliding out a single piece of paper.

Grace's tears fell freely as she unfolded it to read her mother's words:

My little Ballerina, my beautiful girl, Grace,

How I wish that I could be with you today, on what will be your sixteenth birthday.

I owe you an explanation, and an apology, but where do I begin?

I led a charmed childhood until my parents, your grandparents, were killed in a car crash. I did well at school and had just begun college, but when I lost them, I felt so alone. A few months later, I met your father. He was older than me and I now realise that I saw him as a father figure. I fell completely in love with him, was charmed and bewitched by him, and at the age of eighteen, I fell pregnant with you. I was glad!

He wasn't. He had a wife and a daughter – I promise you that I didn't know this – and he chose them. It was as simple as that. I was broken-hearted and I had to give up my career; in short, I was devastated.

For a while after you were born, I was lifted from my depression, so enamoured was I with you; your button nose, your stubby pink fingers and toes and your beautiful smile – you were such a good baby and I loved you so much. But slowly, I sank once again into the depths of despair and was so unwell that I couldn't care for you properly, so I gave you up to the care of my dear Aunt Maud. She never had any children of her own and I knew that she would love you and care for you, and I made her promise that she wouldn't tell you of my treacherous decision.

I think she hated me for what I did, and I certainly hated myself, but I was young and selfish, and also quite unwell. I returned to my studies and continued with my life. It sounds callous but it was the only way that I could survive.

Years later I realised what a fool I had been. I never stopped loving you, Grace, my little ballerina, but I couldn't bring myself to return with the possibility that you would reject me, so instead I wrote you this letter and hoped that when you were sixteen you would find it in your heart to find me and give me the chance to be the mother I wish I could have been to you. I know that I will live my whole life missing you and wishing that I had done things differently,

I love you more than words can say my little ballerina,

Mum (J. M. L)

Grace read the letter again, at first shocked, then angry at her mother's words and the almost flippant recount of her actions. She didn't know whether to be elated that her mother appeared to be still alive, or furious at the way she had behaved, deceiving her for fourteen years and forcing her Great Aunt into complicit silence.

Despite her mother's instructions, she couldn't believe that Maud had kept this from her, her whole life. No wonder she didn't want her to open it until she was two hundred miles away in Richmond. She paced the floor, her emotions all at sea, before flopping down on the bed, exhausted. She needed to speak to Maud.

Down at the office, she asked if she could use the telephone, explaining that she had an important call that she needed to make. The secretary asked her to take a seat and wait for a moment, before making another call, speaking quickly and quietly as she made sidelong glances in Grace's direction.

Almost as soon as she had put down the phone, another door opened and a smartly dressed woman called her name and beckoned her inside.

Once Grace was inside, the woman introduced herself as The Principal and asked if Grace was all right.

"I just need to speak to my aunt." Grace replied, aware that her eyes must be swollen and her face blotchy from crying.

"But you have only just arrived dear, surely she won't

even be home yet."

Grace flopped back into the chair, suddenly feeling defeated.

"This was supposed to be the best day of my life so far, a dream come true, and it has all turned sour. I'm not sure that I can do this, I don't even know who I am anymore."

The principal eyed her keenly. She had delt with many homesick students, but this felt different. "Why don't you tell me what's the matter and then I can take you on a tour of the school and facilities. I'm sure that you will change your mind when you have met the other students and seen what we have to offer here. We would be so sad to lose you before we have even got to know you."

"But I've already seen the school, I was shown round earlier." Grace replied, confusion clouding her face.

"I'm afraid that's not possible, dear, I always show new students around myself."

Grace, however, no longer appeared to be listening. She was staring behind the principle at one of the many photographs of ballerinas on the wall. "It was her," she said, pointing to the picture, "That's the lady that showed me around."

The principle turned to look at the picture, and then slowly turned back to Grace with a strange look on her face.

"I'm afraid that's not possible dear. That is Marguerite de Lacey. She was one of the finest students we have ever had and would certainly have been one of the best in the world, but she died tragically ten years ago. It was a very sad affair, she was let down badly by a man and had to give up her child, and I'm afraid she never got over it."

x

Five years later, on the eve of her twenty first birthday, Grace stepped confidently out onto the stage in her debut performance as a prima ballerina. Her Great Aunt Maud was sitting in the front row looking as proud as any mother, and high above the stage the lights flickered, as the spirit of Marguerite de Lacey watched over her beloved daughter, as she danced what was later to be reported as, 'the greatest ever performance of the Sugar Plum Fairy.'

The Boggart

The treacle-eating Boggart is extremely seldom spied
He shies away from normal folk - their smell he can't abide!
Their lying tongues can boil his blood, he knows their words deride,
so deep below, in boggart holes, he tends to bolt and hide.

The treacle is the reason that their views are not aligned,
for men laid claim to nature's bounty, taking all they found.
From 'neath the hill down snaking tunnels, jewelled chunks were mined,
and processed in the village kitchens - treats of every kind.

Whilst mines provided sweet delights and spicy drinks aplenty,
the lowly Boggart was forgot by workers and the gentry.
Greedily, they claimed their prize until the mine was empty
'til generations long had passed, one hundred years and twenty.

Yet all this time, in quiet preparation, Boggart waited;
a complex maze beneath the hillside, slowly recreated.
He made a map, which faithfully he marked and kept updated,
until at last, a spring he found - the Boggart was elated!

The spring gave birth to viscous streams which slowly pooled to make,
a gooey pond, a sticky cave, a dark and treacly lake.
His secret guarded closely, for he didn't want to wake,
the memories of man, who would, his treasure surely take.

As I Walk

But slowly, surely, as it must, it seeped up to the surface,
until one day it bubbled out - a sticky epidermis.
Thus Boggart, forced to leave his hole, was singular in purpose -
to stem the flow, for if discovered his treacle mine was worthless.

If he was seen, and recognised, he'd sure as sure be followed,
for legend still reminded folk of treacle in the hollows.
A Boggart in the open... and the villagers would know;
they'd hunt him down and find his mine - his home and work exposed.

He left at dusk as night drew in and stayed among the shadows,
and traced the leak, a bubbling pool, to the furthest of the meadows.
With tools, and rocks, he'd ferried there - transported in his barrow,
the spring was plugged - for now at last – supressed beneath the farrows.

But unbeknown, a local lad was camped beside the church,
and when he saw the creature pass his stomach gave a lurch.
He'd quoted village folklore and his words had been besmirched,
and now he vowed to find the mines, from this day he would search.

As years went by the flow was stemmed and kept safe underground,

in caves and tunnels far and wide through every hill and mound.
One day, distracted by his work, and deaf from gurgling sounds,
the Boggart failed to see a shape emerge from sticky ground.

The lad stood silent and observed the strange and eerie sight
of a treacle covered creature, not quite elf or imp or sprite.
With spiky hair and shoulders broad, and squat - with little height,
it's big flat feet and muscled arms assured him of his plight.

But, with a breath he stood up tall, and found his voice to say,
"Hello, I'm William of Wiswell, and I think I've lost my way."
The Boggart turned in disbelief, his thoughts in wild array;
his worst of fears had happened, causing deep and dark dismay.

The Boggart roared, the lad took flight, but couldn't catch his stride;
the slick of treacle caught him fast and caused his feet to slide.
And as the monster fast approached the boy broke down and cried,
his courage gone, bravado quashed, heroic aims belied.

The Boggart picked him up and stood him upright on his feet,
his eyes were sad, his head hung low, his misery complete.
He feared his secret now was known, the treacle would

deplete;
the men would come and mine it all to make their tasty treats.

The Boggart told the boy his fears, he'd nothing left to lose:
How long ago, the men had mined - with greed - and overused!
How he had worked to save the mines, once more to flow and ooze,
to recreate the treacle mines, their sweet and tasty brews.

The boy concurred, a plan was made, the two would work together;
to mine the treacle fairly to be enjoyed by all, forever.
And from that day, the local folk would always have the pleasure
of treacle, sweets and ginger beer, a privilege they'd treasure.

And as for Will of Wiswell and the Boggart - they stayed friends,
and knew that on each other they could certainly depend.
The entrance to the mines remains a secret well defended,
whilst the Boggart - still elusive - lives his treacly life, contented.

Wisp 'o' the Wold

On the edge of the town, in the woods by the stream,
sat the Wisp o' the Wold on a golden sunbeam.
She was watching the damson flies dance on the water,
when into the copse skipped the mill-keepers daughter.

The girl was a wildling, a child of the forest,
her laughter rang free as she ran and she foraged;
snatching at blackberries, apples and sloes
which she popped in her mouth - juicy drips on her clothes.

A wildling she may be, but spoiling the peace
with her noisy intrusions, unnerving the beasts!
With a spirit so strong that the birds fled their nests,
and the squirrels dispersed clutching nuts to their chests.

The Wisp, who was watching, knew just what to do,
she must caution the wildling - that she may leave too!
Just a warning - "Be careful! Play closer to home."
Thus erase this ingrained predilection to roam.

With a swoop and a swirl, and her hair unfurled,
she hurried along to catch up with the girl.

She sped to the treetops and whipped up a storm,
in and out of the branches - a whirlwind was born.
It whistled and screamed in the canopy high,
but the wildling just smiled as she skipped right on by.

With a swoop and a swirl and a furious twirl,
the wisp thought again and caught up with the girl.

As I Walk

She gathered the leaves that had fell to the floor,
made an autumnal cloak the girl couldn't ignore.
As her target approached, she leapt into her path,
but the girl was delighted - immune to her wrath.

With a swoop and a swirl midst the leaves she had hurled,
she was getting quite cross with this fearless young girl.

A different approach; she had words with the grasses,
whose whispering and dancing had spooked lots of lassies.
Happy to help, they performed to their best,
but the girl just sat down to enjoy a small rest.

With a swoop and a swirl Wisp was getting quite vexed,
she had one more idea to get rid of the pest.

She gathered the birds and they all made a plan,
to muster their wild, inner bogey-man.
They awaited their target up high in the branches,
for the signal from Wisp, when they'd start their advances.

The wildling approached, not a care in the world,
unaware of the upset she'd caused in the Wold;
unaware of the army the undergrowth hid;
unaware of their sinister girl-ridding bid.
The starlings descended, a black cloud of feather,
surreal murmuration as they all moved together
The wildling was charmed as this dance she beholded,
and watched open-mouthed as the spectacle unfolded.

Wisp was incensed now, the wildling was tough
and attempts to remove her had not been enough.

As I Walk

The wind and the leaves must once more be harboured -
with the grasses and birds, they must try a lot harder!

A plan was evolving, one final attack;
to unsettle and send the young wildling right back.
They took up positions, got ready for battle,
intent on removing the girl from their chattel.

When all of a sudden, she turned on her heel,
with a clap of her hands and an audible squeal.
For brought on the breeze, down the path, through the woods,
was the smell of her dinner, and it smelled 'oh so good'!

With a swift pirouette she was off like a shot,
skipping back down the path, unaware of their plot.
The wildling was gone and the Wisp was delighted;
as the peace and the calm in the forest was righted.

She returned to the woods, to the copse by the stream,
and relaxed once again on her golden sunbeam.

As I Walk (part 2)

As I walk my mind is free
To think, or not, to just be me
To see the clouds and feel the breeze
                Just following the trail

As I walk, ideas form
I'm not perturbed, this is the norm
Imagination conquers harm
                It is the holy grail

As I walk, I start to write
With words and couplets taking flight
Some have weight, whilst some are light
                But words will never fail

As I walk, a sentence grows
And then another, rhyme or prose
Whilst mind is racing, feet are slow
                And language will prevail

As I walk a tale develops
Rhymes emerge, ideas zealous
Characters and plots envelop
                Wrap me in their veil

I hurry home to write it down
To tweak and tease those verbs and nouns
Manipulate those spoken sounds
                That find me as I walk

As I Walk

As I Walk

About the Author

Diane Neilson is a retired teacher.
Now writing at her leisure, her first stories, songs and poems were written for her own children and grandchildren, and the children she taught.
Since 2021, she has enjoyed writing about her experiences when walking in the English countryside, and the poems she has written for this collection are mostly inspired by the beauty in nature she sees around her every day.
Diane also enjoys writing short stories and has included some in this collection. Her stories are often loosely based around people she has met or experiences she has had, but some are driven by events in the news, and others from a vivid imagination.

Diane also writes travel memoirs, and her first to be published, 'Everybody should walk a Camino' is available in paperback and e-book on Amazon.

As I Walk

As I Walk

Printed in Dunstable, United Kingdom